The Sacred Spot

A Handbook For Sexual Awakening

by Charles & Caroline Muir

This book is part of a 3-piece home study course designed to teach you the basics of Sacred Spot Massage and the healing potential of ancient Tantric art forms. You can enjoy this guide on its own or pair it with its corresponding DVD & 2 CD product. See our website at SourceTantra.com for complete details.

Charles & Caroline Muir

1989   2014

"The Muirs courageously bring to public attention the importance of free-flowing sexual energy for mental and physical well-being; a relationship that much of modern psychology has overlooked. Their sacred spot healing work could be one of the breakthrough healing techniques we've been looking for: a powerful shortcut that involves great pleasure."

- Janna Fineberg, Ph.D. Clinical Psychologist

"Charles Muir originated Sacred Spot Massage in 1978 and now it is a 21st century global movement, found in all neo tantra teachings."

- New Age Magazine

Note: If you have a history of sexual molestation, rape or emotional abuse, seek guidance from a suitable psychological or medical doctor before undertaking this program.

Source School of Tantra Yoga
P.O. Box 368, Kahului, HI 96733
Phone: 888-6-TANTRA (888-682-6872)

Cover Art "Pollenectar" by George Atherton.
See more at www.geoglyphiks.com

Photography by Leah Alchin & Jacob Laren.
Book Design by Jacob Laren.

Published in the United States
by Lulu Press, Inc.

ISBN: 978-1-312-62877-9

For more products, events, seminars and questions answered about Tantra, please visit us online at www.sourcetantra.com!

This work is dedicated to the spirit of the mother, and to the awakening Shakti that resides in all of us.

Acknowledgments

The authors acknowledge the following people for their essential help in making this work possible: J. Michael Kanouff for his many talents and incredible dedication to the art of loving; Mirayam Licht for being an impeccable, multi-faceted Goddess; and Christy, Jacob, Leah and TJ for their willingness to model Tantra for the world.

Leah Alchin for her dedication to Source School of Tantra Yoga and her vital co-teaching of this work; Jacob Laren for managing Source School's business activity; and Christy Flowers Muir for inspiring me with her love, trust, and courage through her own sacred spot healing and awakening.

Sacred Spot Handbook • Table of Contents

Sacred Spot Handbook • Photographs

• SSM = Sacred Spot Massage •

INTRODUCTION
By Caroline G. Muir

At this time in our history, we see the power of the feminine awakening in many ways. Perhaps the most powerful manifestation of this awakening Goddess is the new potential for wholeness in a woman's sexual being.

In this home study course, you will learn techniques to assist in healing the physical, emotional and psychological scars that women have experienced in their lives. These imprints from the past ultimately block the free flow of a woman's orgasmic energy and her power to be all that a woman can be. This multimedia course will provide you with enough information so that you can work with your partner as a team, clearing the blocked and disorganized energy which prohibits the free flow of her sexual energy and her ability to feel great pleasure.

Through this work you will also bring forth the creative energy that in ancient India was known to empower a woman, to bring forth her Goddess-like nature: the priestess, the shaman, the artist, the healer, and the lover that is in every woman.

Sacred spot massage awakens consciousness and

creates magical bonding that enables a couple to grow and love over the course of a lifetime. My own personal experience and experiences of tens of thousands of women in our courses lead me to believe that the sexual healing which results from continued use of sacred spot massage will always yield the same results: an easy, free flow of pleasurable, powerful magical energy; a potential for instantaneous vaginal orgasm and extended multiple orgasm; a youthening process in which the woman becomes more vital, filled with energy and a great glow of self assurance that allows her to blossom in her potential as a healing force on the planet.

As I look back on my own history with sacred spot massage, I know that sharing some of my journey would be helpful to anyone just beginning this transformative practice.

I first encountered this information about 35 years ago at one of Charles' Tantra courses. He had been my yoga and meditation teacher for eight years and when I heard he was teaching techniques of conscious sexuality, I convinced my husband to attend with me. I was already in my third marriage and while I considered our sexual relationship satisfactory I was always left with a lingering feeling that there must be something more to sex than what I had experienced. My husband, as well as my two previous spouses had all at one time or another, asked me "Why don't you want to make love more frequently?" I didn't have an answer.

For 25 years, I found my sexual life frustrating at times. I only knew clitoral orgasms and they were elusive. I would often become frustrated when it seemed that I was going to have a clitoral orgasm, then the feeling disappeared. I felt I had no control as to when I could have one of those wonderful releases of energy.

At my first Tantra class, my husband and I went home and diligently practiced the sacred spot massage. I didn't feel much, and thought that he must be in the wrong area. At times I felt nothing but numbness: at other times a vague soreness and bruised feeling were my only experiences. My husband and I adopted many of the Tantra practices that we learned at our first Tantra course, but dropped sacred spot massage from our life. I felt a little bit like a failure, having heard so many positive stories from other students.

A year later I had left my husband in pursuit of the next "ideal relationship". When that relationship quickly ended, I was left brokenhearted and completely closed down sexually.

Six months later I met Charles in a social situation and somehow found the courage to tell him my story and ask for some of the sexual healing that I knew he taught and practiced. A dear girlfriend of mine had told me her story of how Charles had helped her with her own problems of closing down sexually to men.

I remember going into that first sacred spot session with "the master" thinking that rockets and fireworks would be going off. Instead I experienced periods of pain, irrational fears, crying, a burning sensation and at times an inability to breathe. As a child I had suffered from asthma and remember little of the first six years of my life. As an adult I often suffered from yeast infections and chronic bladder infections and had a complete hysterectomy at age 24.

When I told this to Charles, he said that these were often symptoms of someone who had experienced sexual abuse as a child. I quickly denied any such thing could have happened to me, because I knew my childhood had been perfect even though I couldn't remember it.

Within weeks Charles and I found ourselves growing into relationship, and two years later we were married. Over the last 28 years I have had extensive personal experience with sacred spot massage, and also the opportunity to hear about our students' experiences. Every seminar we teach, I am amazed at the stories of profound healing, awakening and energetic process that our students share with us.

For myself, it took several months for the numbness and pain to begin disappearing from my yoni (the Hindu name for the vagina). The first few times I ejaculated I couldn't even feel it. Little by little my yoni came alive and I began experiencing very powerful vaginal orgasms--not just one, which was all I could ever get out my clitoris, but rather a series of powerful contractions, with pleasure that ran through my entire body.

Within two years my vaginal orgasms were lasting minutes at a time, and with only the shortest of rest periods I could be vaginally orgasmic 30 or 40 times in a session. During this time the Amrita (the Hindu name for female ejaculatory fluid) would gush from my body with each powerful contraction. I was confounded as to where all this incredible nectar could be coming from; I began to believe the tantric writings which stated: "a female's sexual energy is limitless in its potential."

After all these years of sacred spot massage, I do not believe that I have yet found the limit to this incredible energy that God placed inside of Woman. My vaginal orgasms are now easily accessible, the first one usually found within a minute of contact, and I can stay in an extended orgasmic state for as long as I wish. My ejaculate is measured in cupfuls, soaking the towels. I delight in how this journey has transformed me.

The pleasure aspect of the journey has been but a tiny part of the transformation. I have watched myself blossom as a powerful, creative woman. My chronic vaginal infections disappeared after the first year of sacred spot massage. Through a combination of this massage and work with a psychotherapist, I have vividly recalled and cleared many of the childhood psychological scars left by years of sexual, emotional and physical abuse.

My own experiences with this work allow me to personally recommend it to you with great confidence. I urge you to proceed with it gently and patiently!

God bless you on your journey to sexual wholeness. Please write to us and tell us about your experiences.

Caroline Muir
caroline@divine-feminine.com

CHAPTER ONE
Intention

It is important that you both be clear about your goals and intentions for each sacred spot session.

General Intentions

To use these techniques to remove blocks in the woman's sexual energy, and to realign and awaken this energy.

To play together as a team, creating sexual wholeness.

To learn and experiment as two children would, openly and innocently.

To be a perfect receiver or giver, playing only one of these roles.

To awaken consciousness.

To create a special, magical ritual.

Remember this quest is not about giving orgasms, those will come and are simply signposts along the road. You join together here to walk a path, the path of the awakening Shakti, the path of empowerment and healing. Enjoy the journey!

Intention As Receiver

To affirm healing and awakening to take place.

To learn about your shakti energy.

To expand your pleasure, love and energy thresholds. How much can you allow yourself to feel?

To allow deep emotional love to enter your psyche through your yoni.

To allow Goddess to awaken and shine through you.

Intention As Giver

To be there for her, whatever comes up.

To assist her in feeling more loved and special than ever before. To pleasure, heal and honor her.

To let her know how much you care.

To assist her in feeling deeply, emotionally loved through her yoni.

To be a perfect giver, giving in love, instead of giving for love.

CHAPTER TWO
Setting The Mood

It is important to create a special feeling and environment for your initial sacred spot ritual.

Suggestions To The Giver

• Shower, then run a bath for her. While she bathes, set up the bedroom as much like a temple as possible. In subsequent sessions, create this "sacred space" together.

• Bring in some plants or flowers from another room, light candles or soften lighting, put on some relaxing music, set some fruit, chocolate, or a light snack near the bed to serve her later.

• Beautify yourself by dressing up, shaving and grooming.

• Clean, trim and file your nails.

• Turn down the bed, put on special sheets.

• When she comes out from the bathroom, be sitting on the bed in a relaxed and composed position, with your hands in "Namaste".

• Greet her with two sentences of praise and intention. (Such as: "I so look forward to giving to you", "Receive fully, and know I am totally here for you."

• Look lovingly into her eyes as she walks toward you.

• Place a couple of towels under the woman's buttocks, and a pillow under those towels to elevate her slightly. Use other pillows, so both of you are comfortable.

• Heat up the Maui oil and probe.

Suggestions For The Receiver

• Relax and breathe deeply during your bath, ritually purify yourself.

• Beautify yourself.

• Allow yourself to feel like a virgin.

• Empty your bladder completely.

• Go to your healer as a goddess.

CHAPTER THREE
Harmonization of Moods & Energies

Before contacting the woman's second chakra, it is extremely important to first make sure that both of you are energetically and emotionally in harmony. This harmony is created by periods of communication, nurturing, and massage.

Communication

We recommend that you have a short period of talking about feelings. "How are you feeling about all this?"

Ask her to express what her fears, boundaries and intentions are.

Let her share, be a good listener. Let her know you understand and that you really will be there for her. Don't debate or get pulled into a fight.

Nurturing

To practice the nurturing meditation, couples assume the "nurturing position."

They lie together spoon-fashion on their left sides (for energy flow). The receiver on the inside is enveloped in the arms of the giver on the outside.

The purpose of this nurturing position is to create the balance necessary for harmony, to influence a synchronicity between the partners, to adjust their separate energies so that they are vibrating on the same frequency.

Tucked together this way, with their chakras aligned front to back, the two bodies tune one another. Their separate energy centers regulate one to the other, and balance between the partners is achieved.

This meditation can prepare for the intimacy of sacred spot massage, or can allow them a few moments of intimacy in a busy day.

The position will vary slightly from couple to couple because of preferences and the size and shape of the partners, but in all cases comfort is essential. Neither person should experience any strain or persist in a position of the slightest discomfort.

With the giver holding the woman, his right hand should rest on her heart chakra, between the breasts; his left arm should slip under the crook of her neck (the weight of his head borne by a pillow so his arm is free to move) and his left hand should rest on her forehead (sixth chakra) or on top of her head (seventh chakra).

Nurturing Position • Receiver In Front

As you lie together, close your eyes and relax. Quiet your mind by focusing on deep breathing. Concentrate on the path of your breath as it rises up into--and the down out of--your nostrils. After awhile, become aware of your partner's breath.

Two breathing techniques are performed in this position:

The first, used during the beginning of the meditation, is called the harmonizing breath: the couple inhales together, holds the breath together, exhales together, and holds the breath out together. During this harmonizing breath the woman is the receptive body, accepting energy through the back and into the chakras, filling up with that energy on each inhalation and discharging downward on the exhalation. The partner on the outside is the giver, and should emphasize each exhalation, projecting the chakras' energy from the front of the body into the receptive back side of the beloved. Practice three whole breaths (inhaling, holding in, exhaling, holding out) at each chakra, beginning at the heart center.

Focus attention on navel chakra next, then on the brow chakra. From there concentrate on the sexual chakra.

It is important for both partners to focus on the same chakra region at the same time. The giver should move the lower hand from heart to navel and second chakra to facilitate this focus and increase the energy.

The second breathing technique, used during the second part of the nurturing exercise, is called the reciprocal charging breath. This time one partner breathes in as the other partner breathes out. In this way, during the several seconds that the breath is held, one partner will be holding the breath in, the other holding the breath out. As you practice the reciprocal charging breath, be conscious of the energy your partner is imparting to you as well as the energy you are giving back. This weaves the two partner's energies together.

The nurturing meditation allows couples to communicate on at least three levels: on the physical level (body to body), on the more subtle respiratory level (breath to breath), and on the most subtle level (chakra to chakra). Over time such regular communication creates a kind of synergy between the partners' chakras.

The focus on breath and energy centers seems to create its own energy. Certainly when partners complete this meditative posture, they each hold more energy than when they first joined together.

When you have completed this meditation (it should last five to ten minutes), use another tantric means of communication before you go on to sacred spot massage. Look into one another. Don't speak; just gaze upon the face of your partner with whom you now feel so well connected.

Notice the light that radiates from your lover's eyes; it is another by-product of the nurturing meditation, the light of love when harmony exists.

Massage & Bodywork

To further prepare the woman for her energetic journey, and to bring her more fully into her body, a short massage is next. If you have no experience in massage we recommend you obtain one of the many fine videos or books on massage that are available.

Learning to give each other a massage is one of the great things couples can do to ensure a feeling of nurturing and value. The health, relaxation and increased energy that mutual massage provides is well worth any effort it takes. Here are some general guidelines for sensual massage.

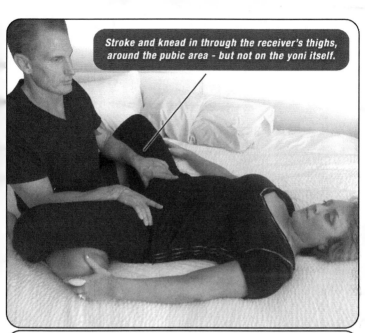

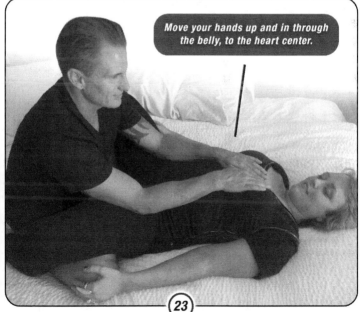

23

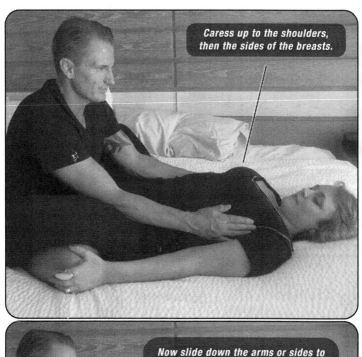

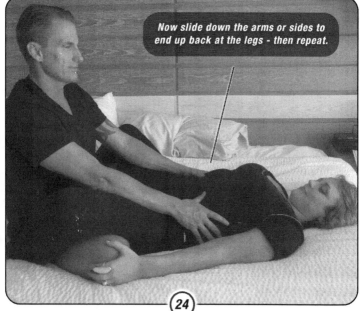

After several minutes of this you can come closer to the yoni with your strokes, lightly titillating without any overt sexual gestures. Work in through the belly and see if there are any cramped areas, which can be relieved through gentle, firm pressure as the woman exhales. Gradually make the massage more sensual, including clitoral stimulation.

CHAPTER FOUR
Positions For Sacred Spot Massage

Here are some suggested positions for doing sacred spot massage. You may create other positions as you become familiar with these.

Woman squatting.

Lying side by side position.

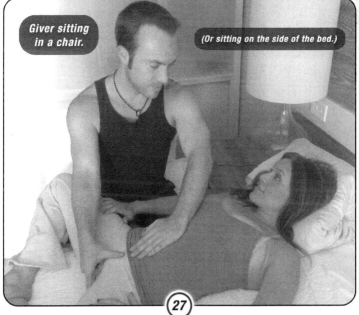

Giver sitting in a chair.

(Or sitting on the side of the bed.)

Woman sitting on the giver's lap.

Important Points To Remember:

1) New positions should allow contact of the giver's palm to the receiver's pubic mound and clitoris.

2) Eye contact is very important. The giver should have their eyes open, and the receiver should have her eyes open at least half the time.

3) Comfort for both partners is essential. Use pillows, chairs, walls, the headboard and anything else you like to assist in this.

4) Change positions periodically, so you never get tired or strained.

CHAPTER FIVE
Contacting The Second Chakra

Tantric writings describe the female second chakra as having two magnetic poles of energy and pleasure.

The External Pole - The Clitoris

Before entering the yoni to contact the sacred spot, there should be a period of activating the shakti through touching the clitoris.

We want to address the clitoris in a very, very gentle way that is more yin than ever before.

Many women like yang stimulation, but the real power and pleasure potential of the clitoris can be brought out through the yin - through light touch, slow touch, and especially through a finger or tongue that is very limp; soft rather than rigid or hard.

Three Qualities of Yin & Yang

Yin: Slow Movement, Light Pressure, Limp Fingers / Tongue, Short Strokes, Cool, Left Hand, Magnetic Negative

Yang: Fast Movement, Hard Pressure, Stiff Fingers / Tongue, Long Strokes, Hot, Right Hand, Magnetic Positive

Touch all around the clitoris, especially the side of the shaft which has "roots" going down at least an inch in depth. Gentle pressure and stroking of the inner and outer lips which are anatomically part of the clitoris.

You can suggest to the woman that she take your fingers in her hand, and gently massage her clitoris with them. Lubricate your fingers with some high-quality natural oil meant for external use, such as Maui Moisturizing Body Oil (see sourcetantra.com).

Ask the receiver to tell you when she likes something; encourage her to feel free to make suggestions as to what she would enjoy.

The woman can maintain contact with the clitoris at any time during the session

The Internal Pole - The Sacred Spot

Before entering the yoni, the giver should look into the eyes of the woman and ask, "May I enter your sacred space?" This is an important part of the ritual at the beginning of every round.

Lubrication can be energetically and sensually enhancing. Too much friction can cause the area to numb out. We recommend a product called Probe Personal Lubricant for internal massage (see sourcetantra.com).

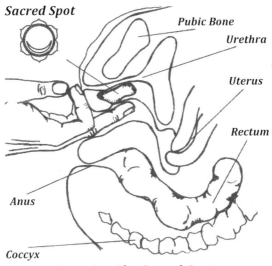

Locating The Sacred Spot

To locate the Sacred Spot, begin with the ring finger, which has an energetic harmony with the second chakra. You may switch to the middle finger after about seven minutes. Eventually you can access the sacred spot with both fingers, usually in round 3 of the session.

Insert the finger(s) straight into the yoni, as far back as it goes, toward the cervix. This is not the sacred spot area, but do this initially as a locator. You then curl the finger(s) back toward yourself in a sort of "come here" gesture all the way forward to the front wall of the vagina, behind the lower pubic bone.

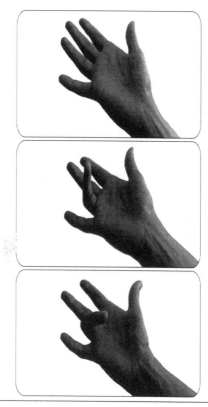

Hold the contact without movement, letting the receiver's consciousness meet your finger(s). After one minute begin linear stroking, experimenting with yin and yang qualities.

Gradually proceed to these other strokes, painting the entire area

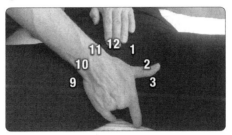

LINEAR - From upper pubic bone down to lower pubic bone. Using a clock face as a reference point, start at 12:00 and stroke downward to 6:00, then 11:00 downward to 7:00 and then continuing across to 1:00 downward to 5:00.

CRESCENT - Use wrist motion to gently inscribe a crescent, making sure that the giver's palm is lightly touching the clitoris and vagina lips.

PRESSING - Press on the receiver's exhalation and out-held breath: giver releases pressure as receiver inhales. Make a grid of the entire area internally and remember "hot" spots.

PULSING - Tapping different points on and around the perimeter of the sacred spot.

VIBRATING - Loose finger(s) in a gentle side to side motion.

CIRCULAR - Clockwise and counter-clockwise from the wrist.

DIAGONAL - Rotate the wrist so finger(s) start at 1:00 and go across to 7:00. Then reverse 11:00 to 5:00.

After trying these strokes in their yin and yang expressions, make a dance of all of them. Remember to be totally still periodically.

When you confront painful areas, go into them together gently, for 10 seconds. You don't have to go too deeply into the sore spots, just deep enough to feel them and to own them.

Remember to map out the pleasurable areas and the painful or numb areas. Make pathways from pleasurable areas to tender areas and vice versa.

The giver should experiment with changing the hand or finger positions when contacting very tender spots. The left and right hand as well as each finger have a different quality of energy. For this reason the giver should learn to be ambidextrous in this type of massage.

In round three when the receiver feels ready, enter the yoni with the ring and middle fingers as shown below:

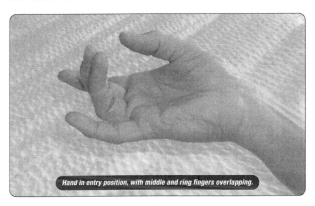

Hand in entry position, with middle and ring fingers overlapping.

Bring the two fingers as close together to overlapping as possible, so that the padded part of the middle finger comes over the nail of the ring finger.

Remember to play with the yin and yang. Sometimes go a little faster, sometimes a little slower. Sometimes create more pressure with the hand, sometimes less. Explore all along the area from 11 to 1 o'clock and downward from 5 to 7 o'clock, holding attention in your fingers, and be mindful of the receiver's face.

Watch for facial expressions of pain or emotions. Monitor the receiver's breathing also. Holding her breath will short circuit her energy. Connected breathing assists in moving blocked energy and emotions. Remind her to breathe if she stops, or to "sound" if her yoni is tender.

There may occasionally be pain, emotions, bruised feelings or burning. Whenever this occurs, it's good to honor the receiver's boundaries by stopping the massage and using mudras. After several sessions, when you're both comfortable with this type of massage, it is okay to go into the pain, in a conscious and gentle way, stretching the boundaries that may just be limitations ready to fall away.

Ritual sessions should last between 90 and 120 minutes, and should be broken down into three or four rounds, with a cuddle break between them. This allows for energetic and psychological integration.

CHAPTER SIX
Mudras

In your sacred spot massage, you will be interspersing approximately 10 minute periods of the "active massage" learned in the last chapter, with periods of "passive holds" called Mudras. Mudras are hand positions which affect energy on a very subtle and profound level.

Mudras reorganize energy that has become disorganized due to life experiences and conditioning. They assist in moving blocked energy that is deeply seated. These are usually emotional blocks, rather than physical.

Mudras are also used to alter the flow of the energy, so it can be made to move in an accelerated speed or in a direction opposite to its normal polarity.

When sexual energy is made to move upwards, it awakens consciousness and regenerates the entire organism.

The mudras work with principles of energy which state that the first five chakras (running from the tail bone to the throat) each generate a specific dominant quality of energy, which because of their density, are given an elemental recognition.

These energies connect with the five fingers of each hand.

For the base chakra it is the energy of earth and this energy channels out through the little finger.

The ring finger has to do with the water element, and has an energetic connection to the second chakra.

The middle finger connects with the third chakra and the fire element.

The index finger connects with the heart chakra and its air element.

The thumb, the ether element, connects to the throat center.

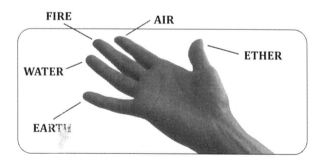

Chakra Locations:	Yantra:	Element & Finger:	Bija Tone:	Psychological Drive:
7-Cranial Crown of head		—	Aum sound	—
6-Occipital Third eye between eye brows		—	("au" for 6, "mmm" for 7)	—
5-Cervical Spine Jugular notch of throat		Ether Thumb	Ham	Spiritual
4-Thoracic Spine Center of chest between nipples		Air Index finger	Yam	Love
3-Lumbar Spine Behind navel		Fire Middle finger	Ram	Power
2-Sacral Spine Inside & external to reproductive organs		Water Ring finger	Vam	Sex
1-Coccyx Inside & external to anus		Earth Little finger	Lam	Material needs

Here are some beginner and intermediate mudras. We suggest you learn advanced mudras and other advanced practices from a Certified Tantra Educator (C.T.E.). See sourcetantra.com for a list of our certified teachers.

Uniting The Energy Poles

The giver puts the paddy part of the thumb lightly upon either side of the shaft of the clitoris, while the middle finger is inside the yoni on the sacred spot.

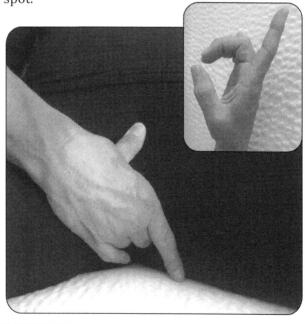

Visualization:

This mudra uses the mind to imagine, feel, or visualize that the energy from the finger on the sacred spot connects with the thumb on the clitoris. With each exhalation, send energy out the finger to the thumb. As you breathe in, you create a circuit between those two fingers, as if you would energetically create a spark or a connection between them on the exhalation.

In subsequent sessions the giver can alternate static holds with very gentle stimulation to the sacred spot while he maintains the clitoral contact. The woman can put her hand over the giver's thumb, and gently rock the hand or vibrate it as she sees fit. But for the first few sessions, only use a static hold.

It's important for you to know that if you change the finger contacting the sacred spot (if your ring finger or index finger, for instance, is on the sacred spot rather than the middle finger) it is a different mudra. It will be a different energetic and will have a subtle but different effect. You should play with all of the finger combinations over a period of time, including using either combination of two fingers (index finger and middle finger, or middle finger and ring finger) on the sacred spot with the thumb on the clitoris, too. Each finger combination is a different mudra, so "uniting the energy poles" is actually five different mudras.

Foundation Mudra

The next several mudras all use this same hand position as a foundation. We will refer to it as the foundation mudra from now on.

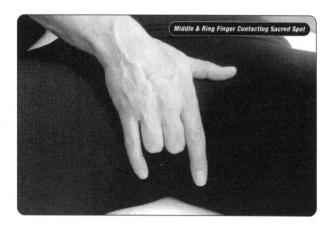

The hand contacts the yoni, with either of the 3 middle fingers (or any combination of 2), curled on the sacred spot. The oiled palm of the hand goes against the clitoris and the rest of the palm conforms to the external mound of the vagina.

Uniting The Hands

Insert one hand in the yoni using the foundation mudra. The other hand is going to find the pubic bone in the lower abdomen. Just above the pubic bone, gently push inward and downward toward the sacred spot. If there is a lot of resistance, tightness in the muscle, pain or cramping, it should be a lighter pressure.

One hand contacts the sacred spot inside, the other gently pushes down toward it.

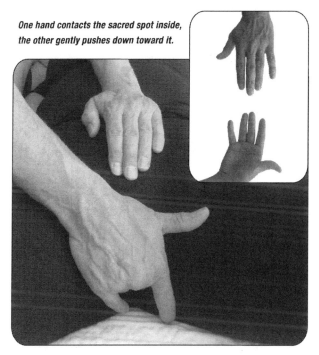

Visualization:

From your heart send your loving energy out the hand that's in the yoni, up to the area just above the pubic bone and belly. Send energy out the hand as you exhale, catching it in the other hand (the one externally above the pubic bone) as you inhale.

Connecting Passion With Love

Many women find it very difficult to feel both sexy and intimate at the same time. This mudra transforms that condition, so that shakti and heart energy unite in their highest expression.

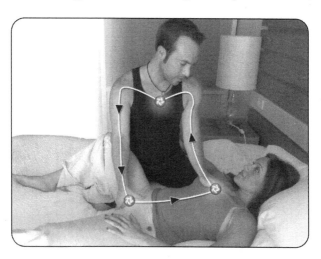

Visualization:

One hand in Foundation Mudra, the other hand lightly on the chest between the breasts. As the giver breathes in, they should "catch" the energy in the hand that's on the receiver's heart. Allow your own energy to come into the left hand, up your left arm to the shoulder, down from the shoulder into the heart center from whence it originated.

As the giver exhales, imagine, feel or visualize that you send energy from your heart up to the right shoulder, down the arm and out the right hand, into her yoni. Your energy runs into her yoni, up through the center of her body, to where your left hand is on her heart. It completes the circuit by going up your left arm back to your heart, where it is again imprinted with your love and intention, ready to again be sent out with your exhalation (follow arrows).

Clearing Abuse

It is estimated by noted psychological authorities that over 30% of all children were abused sexually, emotionally and/or physically. In the 35 years we have been teaching this work, this mudra for some unknown reason has helped many people recall incidents of abuse and has helped many victims clear the energetic imprint locked in the psyche, so that sexual wholeness could finally be theirs.

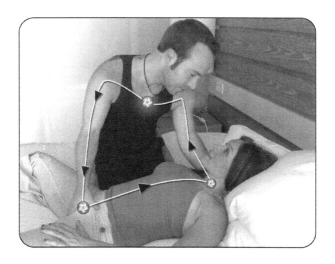

The lower hand in the Foundation Mudra and the upper hand under the back of the neck to the area between fourth and fifth cervical vertebra. Run the energy between your hands. Experiment with first left and then right hands in the yoni, and with different finger combinations; there are different responses to different energies. The receiver's sounding and emotional toning on the exhalation are very important in this mudra, as is connected breathing.

Visualization:

"Run" the energy from the right hand (follow the arrows), through the receiver's body, up to the left hand.

Connecting Passion With Spirit

In ancient times, it was understood that sexual energy was the fuel that ignited the process of spiritual enlightenment. Western conditioning has imprinted most of us with layers of guilt, fear and shame, leaving us not knowing how to be both a sexual being and a spiritual being at the same time.

This mudra allows us to recollect our innocence, and experience the true spiritual nature of sexual energy. It also opens energy and nerve pathways between the mind and sexual centers.

The lower hand in foundation mudra and the other hand with the thumb pressing the brow center (the area between the eyes and slightly above), and the other four fingers touching just beyond the hairline to the front fontanelle. The eyes of the giver and the receiver should be periodically connected throughout the mudra - though you can both try closing your eyes as well.

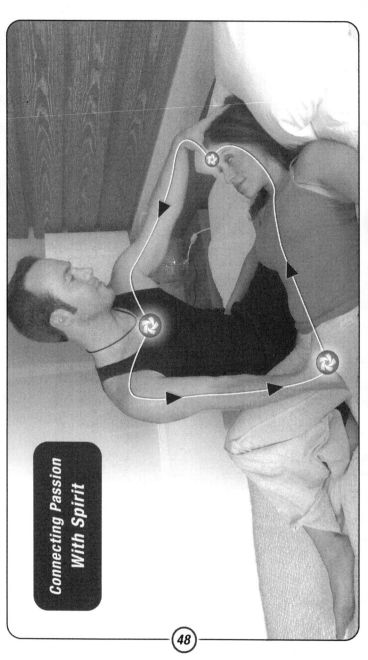

Connecting Passion With Spirit

Visualization:

Run energy from the lower hand to the upper (follow arrows), with the thought or affirmation "Awaken".

Other Easy Mudras

Other easy mudras have the lower hand in the Foundation Mudra, with any one finger or combination of fingers on the sacred spot. The other hand can come either to the underside of the back of the heart or the navel, the underside of the back of the brain opposite the third eye, or underneath the sacrum. Use a static hold and run the energy current between the right and left hands.

Visualization:

Send the energy into the yoni on your exhalation, catching your own energy in the other hand on the inhalation, thus connecting the chakras energetically.

When the upper hand is on the front of the chakra the mudra tends to be more opening in nature. When it is on the back of the body it tends to be more cleansing.

Important Points to Remember
When Doing Mudras

1) Alternate periods of massage with mudras. This allows the receiver's psyche to assimilate and reorganize the energy which the massage releases.

2) Changing the finger contact on the sacred spot will change the energy of the mudra; different fingers access different energies and parts of the receiver's psyche.

3) Use mudras on sore spots in the yoni when massage doesn't seem to relieve the pain, or when the receiver is resistant to how the massage feels.

4) Energy follows consciousness - run the energy between the hands or fingers. Imagine, feel, affirm and/or visualize this taking place.

5) As you practice the mudras, both of you should alternate periods of eyes open and eyes closed to see which combination is most effective.

6) Mudras should be held for 45-90 seconds of total stillness.

CHAPTER SEVEN
Tips For The Giver

Let go of all your expectations and desires as to what should happen in the session. It's her special time.

Whatever happens, let her know "it's okay" and you're there for her.

The most important thing during this massage is not how versed you are in the massage strokes, or how beautiful you are or how sexy, and it's really not even about how many orgasms you can give her in a session; **it is the giving, the atmosphere you create, the safety, the being there and your loving heart presence that are most important to the woman.**

Empower her to give you any feedback about what she's feeling.

Any time you find a painful spot, map it in your mind's eye for future reference and visit it in subsequent sessions.

Always observe and monitor the quality of the tissue beneath your hands. Observe how the muscles are feeling and what's going on with her energetically as well as emotionally.

Make sure she's not holding her breath, and gently remind her to breathe if she's not.

Periodically maintain a light pressure and gentle stroking with your other hand on her clitoris' shaft, and inside and outside of her vaginal lips.

Suggest she just rest her hands on her clitoris and heart chakra during the massage.

Periodically compliment and praise her; also assure her that you're having a good time and that you love being there for her.

Mix the energies of yin and yang massage and periodically mix in a mudra.

Shine your light into her pain and numbness.

If she gets sexually excited, do not go for orgasms - let them come to you if they want.

When orgasms or female ejaculation (amrita) are happening, continue steady stroking, do not "rev up" the pressure or speed.

CHAPTER EIGHT
Tips For The Receiver

Ultimately, your task in sacred spot massage is how much love, pleasure and feeling you can allow yourself to take in through your yoni - your sacred space.

Don't perform, just "be".

Get out of your own way and let it happen.

Your ability to receive is the ultimate gift that you can give to the giver.

The release of great orgasmic energy involves you giving up control. Trust the giver to hold that space for you and let yourself merge with the energy.

Feel the tingles of energy, then the ripples and finally the waves of the shakti energy flowing throughout your entire body. Breathe the sensation upwards to your brain. Feel the potential of its power. Allow it to bring forth all that you are as woman and as a true Goddess Awakening.

It's important for you to keep your eyes open at least half of the time.

Meditate on your energy, your feelings, and your experience. Watch your mind and take note of where it wanders.

Don't "trance out" or disassociate.

When you want to close down, instead let the giver's love and energy in.

Toning and making sound prevents headaches, and activates the vagus nerve for more pleasure.

Suppressed rage numbs passion, so bellow your rage out, but not at the giver.

Relax into any unpleasant feelings.

Rest your right hand on the clitoris and your left hand on your breasts during this massage. It's OK to pleasure your clitoris during the massage, but do not go for orgasm.

Periodically dance on the giver's hand; don't just lay passively.

Signs of enough energy for a given session: heat in spine, chills, intense fear.

Watch your dreams for several nights after sacred spot sessions. They often will be revealing and assist in further cleansing and healing.

Take a look at the barriers and the limits you put up around how much pleasure you allow yourself to feel. Drop those barriers. If you have an orgasm, it's just the gateway to waves of orgasm, to many orgasms and extended orgasm - a joyful, easy release of energy coming to you in the future as you grow more and more whole with each sacred spot session.

Whatever you are feeling physically or emotionally, breathe it up to your brain on your inhalation and make up a sound for what you are feeling on the exhalation. This will create new neural pathways between body and brain, along with integration of past, present and the future which already is.

CHAPTER NINE
Tips About Process

Tantricas understand that relationship yields the possibility that great healing and awakening will take place for each individual. They also recognize that relationship has the potential to push buttons that previous relationships have set up.

Because the second chakra is an emotionally based chakra, you will sometimes come into contact with layers of deeply seated emotions that will trigger emotional process - process being defined as the receiver not fully in the present time, but instead feeling emotions connected to some experience of her past.

It is important for the giver to be able to sense when the woman is in process, as early as possible.

These are some of the things to look for: Her breathing pattern will change; it may quicken or she may stop breathing. You might see rapid eye movement behind her closed eyes. You may notice that her eyes have stayed closed a little too long. Her facial muscles may tighten into a grimace.

She'll express an intense desire to "just want to stop now."

She may have so many feelings that she cannot identify them.

She may go into emotional patterns that are more congruent with being a child rather than an adult; this child may speak to you in blaming ways or catty ways.

She may feel and/or discharge heavy emotional energy.

Emotional Issues That May Come Up:

She can't trust you
She doesn't think you'll be there for her
Suppressed rage
Fear
Guilt
Shame
Unworthiness
Abortion issues
Molestation/rape issues

As the giver, when you detect the receiver going into process, you must switch into "Process Mode" remembering these points:

1. Be a knight in shining armor. Christ-like.

2. Take nothing she says personally, even if it's said to you in a blaming manner.

3. Pretend that the you she is attacking, is different than the you who is there giving to her.

4. Do not take on the blame; do not try to fix her and make it better.

5. Intensify your "being there" and let her talk, honoring everything she says.

6. Remember that none of her emotionally based communications have to make sense. They don't have to be truth and fact based.

7. Ask her to share more with you, and listen to her; don't solve, correct, defend or interrupt.

8. There's a hurt little girl inside that processing woman. With what gentleness would you speak to a child so they can hear you?

9. A good mantram to say to her is, "I understand how you can feel that way. I'm here for you now. Take my love in."

Process Tips For The Giver

1. Stop all sacred spot massage during these moments.

2. Maintain the contact on the sacred spot with a mudra and simply hold her.

3. Maintain your loving eye gaze and look into her left eye especially. Look in and see the little girl that is captured in that woman's body. Suggested mantrams: "I'm here for you now. Come on, let's feel this together".

4. Whatever happens, let her know it's okay that it is happening.

5. Invoke and evoke the divine, however the two of you perceive God/Goddess.

6. Allow something higher than yourself to come through you.

7. Your job is just to assist her in unwinding emotionally. Support her with loving energy and the emotions will unwind.

8. If tears are there, thank her for the tears.

9. When it's time to resume massage, if there have been areas of great pleasure that you've

discovered in her yoni, go to those areas. Build up a pleasant feeling and energy, then make a pathway, sliding your hand over to the painful area. Do a little massage and mudra in the painful area, and again slide back to the pleasant area thus connecting the pleasure spots to the sore spots.

Process Tips For The Receiver

Accept that there may be process and delight in it. Do not be upset at yourself if you feel that you can't trust your partner, or if other heavy emotional issues come up. Remember, even though he may have pushed those buttons over the lifetime you've been together, those patterns were set up earlier in your life.

The walls you hit are so important! You must first find them before you can go through them in a later session. There is always a door in the wall!

Feel whatever it is you're feeling and as you feel it, stay connected with the giver; open your eyes and take in their loving gaze, because whatever you experienced in the past you've likely experienced alone. Here you have a chance to access that experience, taking in the love of the giver, and together as a team bring in love, consciousness and energy to what you experienced in the past. By taking in the love present-time and directing it to what you are feeling - the feeling being based on something you experienced in the past - there is a likelihood that you can energetically resolve that past experience, and be free of it in your future.

Remember, you don't have to remove a whole lifetime of imprints in one session. Enjoy the journey.

It is important for the receiver to continue to breathe throughout this session. Many women short circuit their orgasmic energy by unconsciously holding their breath.

Communicate your needs and feelings to the giver in a non-blaming way.

Do not be afraid to invoke and evoke whatever your belief system allows in the way of angelic forces, inner essence, inner guides, God in heaven, Mother, whatever fits your belief system. Call on that which is Holy to imprint this chakra temple.

CHAPTER TEN
Subsequent Sessions

After your initial ritual, use a short period of sacred spot massage as a part of your regular sexual loving. In addition, once every week or two, create another extended ritual session lasting at least an hour.

After you have a month or two of experience with the previous chapter's information, you may begin practicing and gently playing with the following intermediate techniques.

Giver:

Using the yin tongue on the clitoris while the finger contacts the sacred spot is a powerful combination. Alternate periods of stimulating first the clitoris and then the sacred spot. This simultaneously activates the pudendal and pelvic nerve pathways, up to the brain.

Receiver:

If you've had experience with rebirth type breathing, yogic panting breath, Grof breathing, or with joyous breath release, these are excellent types of breathing to utilize whenever big energy builds up, whenever there's numbness, process, or whenever there's tenderness and tightness in the yoni. This type of breathing has you pulling the breath in, either through your nose or your mouth, and then letting it just fall out on the exhalation and immediately connecting the exhale to the next inhale, and so on.

Both partners can sound or tone together, as you keep eye contact. This is especially powerful during orgasm.

Try very slow crescent strokes with pressure down both sides of the yoni from 12:00 to 6:00, clockwise, and with the other hand from 12:00 to 6:00 counter-clockwise.

The receiver can pulse and squeeze her vaginal muscles against the giver's fingers, while the giver contacts any painful spot.

The receiver can become the active partner, dancing on the giver's fingers, while the giver holds static contact on tender spots.

The receiver should make sounds or tones when she feels stuck energy, emotions or extreme physical tenderness (bruised feelings, burning sensations). Make up a sound to describe the feeling.

The receiver may rock by pushing against the bedboard or wall with her feet. She may dance on your fingers, pushing her feet down on the bed and moving as if she were "taking your hand" or massaging your fingers rather than being massaged.

The giver may gently rock the woman by placing a hand under her sacrum, while the sacred spot hand remains still.

Givers, should the woman release orgasm, there are several things you should do:

Feel that release of orgasm; as you breathe in, allow it to be absorbed by your entire body and especially by the hand that's in the yoni.

Make a positive statement while the receiver orgasms; affirmations and visualizations are greatly empowered when you join them to sexual energy. When a person releases orgasm, their psyche is opened dramatically and these moments are potentially magical in their transformative effect. Here are some suggested affirmations with the power of mantrams:

> "You are so powerful!"
> "You are so beautiful!"
> "I love you so much!"

"I see Goddess in you!"
"Awaken!"
"May this energy heal and awaken you!"
"The past is over! You are whole now!"
"I love you forever!"
"Your yoni is a temple!"

In all mudras, the receiver can breathe in while the giver breathes out, and vice versa. When this harmonization breath, taught in Chapter 3, is joined to mudras, it amplifies the power and effect of the mudra.

To further amplify the energy, the giver can visualize pulling their own energy up from their 2nd chakra, up to their heart on the inhalation, and then sending that energy out the hand in the yoni on the exhalation.

These last three techniques are advanced and should be used only after you both have lots of sacred spot massage experience, or in the presence of a Certified Tantric Educator (C.T.E.).

For a free listing of our Source Tantra CTEs, see sourcetantra.com.

CHAPTER ELEVEN
Final Considerations

Whether it takes a month or a year of playing with this information, the outcome will be more wholeness in your yoni, more pleasurable energy for both of you to play with, and more power to use in transformative ways in the world.

At the same time you will experience an increasing sense of harmony - within yourselves, your family, and in your world.

You'll be able to look back each month of your life and see the changes unfold. You will feel the depth of the bonding and trust you are creating.

You will also be able to feel and observe how the pain or numbness disappears gradually and is replaced by an ability to deeply feel the energy, the bliss, the love, the shakti, the sacredness of your yoni space, and the goddess that is in every woman.

Enjoy the journey!

With Love,
Charles & Caroline Muir

TANTRIC GLOSSARY
A Language Of Love

Amrita: The ancient Hindu name for female ejaculatory fluid.

Bandha: Techniques of internal muscular locks which bind energy, increasing its build up and influencing its flow.

Bija Mantram: Vibratory tones that are seed syllables to awaken and affect energy in a positive fashion.

Chakra: Generators and reservoirs of energy and consciousness. In the Hindu tradition there are seven of them located along the spinal column from the base of the tail bone to the crown of the head.

Lingam: The male sexual organ, wand of light.

Mantram: Words, tones, or statements with transformative power.

Mudra: Hand and/or body positions utilized to influence subtle energies in transformative fashion.

Nadi: Conduits that conduct energy throughout the body.

Namaste: Greetings, I bow to the Light that resides within you. A prayerful hand position.

Sacred Space: The vagina of a woman who has realized her sexual center is a temple whose energy and space is Holy.

Sacred Spot: An internal and external access point to the core of the second chakra's energy, and the sexual psyche.

Shakti: The creative female energy which is spiritual energy that is sexually based.

Tantra: An expansive weaving of energy which is a path to Self Realization. Sexual yoga is but one of the forms of Tantra.

Tantrica: One who practices Tantra.

Yang: The positive, magnetically charged energy; hot in nature, it expresses itself in many forms which are often described as masculine in nature.

Yantra: Geometric shapes that when visualized or gazed at, affect energy and assist the practitioner in the manifestation of their will. The yantras for the seven chakras assist the practitioner in harmonizing, awakening and accelerating the energy of the seven chakras, as they simultaneously awaken the dormant consciousness inherent in each chakra.

Yin: The negative, magnetically charged energy; cool in nature, it expresses itself in many forms which are often described as feminine in nature.

Yoga: Union of the highest nature.

Yoni: Sacred space; the female sexual center which is a temple of light, energy, healing and life.

FURTHER TEACHINGS
The Next Step On Your Journey

After practicing with this booklet and its associated materials, you may want to deepen your mastery in Tantra. There are a number of products we recommend you investigate, as well as a series of seminars we offer for in-person instruction. If you feel called to join us down the path, don't hesitate!

If you have any questions about any of our products or seminars, call 888-6-TANTRA or e-mail school@sourcetantra.com.

ULTIMATE DVD COLLECTION
5 DVD Set - Store Price $150
See sourcetantra.com:
ONLINE ONLY SPECIAL $55

INCLUDED DVDs:

Sexual Healing: The Tantra Way DVD
This educational, profound and often humorous DVD presents renowned Tantra Master, Charles Muir, addressing over 100 of the world's leading Tantra educators and sexual healers.

Secrets of Female Sexual Ecstasy DVD

This educational, erotic, and exceptionally beautiful DVD from Charles and Caroline Muir will show you ways to more intimacy, passion, and emotional connection than you can now imagine. Explicit yet not X-rated, sexual loving is depicted with an innocence, beauty, and wisdom that transforms sex into a new art form for the 21st century, with clear instructions to awaken and release unlimited orgasmic energy.

Meeting of the Masters 3 DVD Set

These DVDs feature Tantra Master Charles Muir and Taoist Grandmaster Mantak Chia teaching together across a wide array of topics centering on the power of sexual energy.

Volume 1: Alchemy, Orgasm & Awakening

The foremost teachers of Tantra and Tao come together to teach the art of sacred sexuality that originated in ancient India and China.

These secrets have time and again proven highly effective in increasing sexual vitality and thus creating a younger, healthier body.

Volume 2: Sex, Energy & Ecstatic Love

• Practices for singles, couples and same sex partners
• Principles of directing energy
• Using sexual energy for spiritual awakening
• Orgasms, ingasms and sex magic
• Regenerative practices in masturbation
• Instruction in Taoist exercises and meditations

Volume 3: Eastern Secrets of Sexual Love

• Powerful Sexual Chi Gung Practices & Techniques
• Compassion Fire Breathing Meditation Technique
• Energy Organ Wrapping For Healing & Rejuvenation
• Ejaculatory Control & Full Body Orgasm Techniques
• Educating Your Children About Sacred Sexuality

White Tantra Yoga (Laya Yoga) harnesses the power of your love, breath, and mind, directing it towards your chakras and body. It is a form of Kundalini Yoga which alternates the moving meditation of stretching with periods of profound sitting meditations.

Yogi Charles Muir, accompanied by award-winning New Age musicians, expertly guides you through this form of self love, self regeneration, and self realization. These productions are great for beginners and advanced Hatha Yoga students. They are a vital part of any Tantric practice.

DELUXE CRYSTAL WAND
Self Use or With Partner - $40

See sourcetantra.com
to order yours today!

Now you can practice sacred spot massage on your own if you don't have a partner.

This 10 inch sensuously curved crystal (1/2" inch diameter) Lucite G Spot Stimulator and Prostate Massage Tool is individually made for your pleasure and awakening. The hard Lucite provides firm stimulation that our many users rave about!

The Crystal Wand is even a beautiful erotic art piece on its own! The S shaped design gives you the needed leverage to easily find and reach the G Spot (sacred spot) and prostate (Male G Spot) for effortless self stimulation.

MAUI MASSAGE OIL
The Hawaiian Love Oil - $20

See sourcetantra.com
to order yours today!

ALL NATURAL OIL

Treat your partner to the best! This erotic and exotic love oil is rich in natural vitamins and contains no artificial ingredients or preservatives.

This is the perfect lubricant for external genital stimulation. Maui Moisturizing Body Oil – The Hawaiian Love Oil, actually enhances your partner's touch, making it more erotic, sensual and healing. As a non-greasy compound, it is our personal formulation of the finest avocado, apricot, coconut, macadamia, jojoba, and vitamin

E oils. Rich in natural vitamins, it is also the most luxurious massage oil you will ever use.

Our large 8 ounce bottle is enough for several sessions of massaging your partner head to toe!

PROBE PERSONAL LUBRICANT
Silky & Light 8.5oz - $15
17oz Bottle - $19.50

See sourcetantra.com
to order yours today!

Designed to emulate a woman's natural lubrication, Probe® is the best, most natural lubricant on the market. It has three simple ingredients, no harsh chemicals, fragrance-free, and a natural citrus preservative.

Probe is safe for vaginal and rectal use. It is harmless if swallowed. It will not irritate, nor cause yeast or bacterial infections. It is strongly recommended by health professionals and sacred spot massage originator Charles Muir.

Visit our website today to see our complete Tantra store that contains all of these products and many more to help you down your path! Sourcetantra.com

TANTRA SEMINARS
Experiential Events For Mastery

While home-study materials are a great start to your journey, we also offer a number of weekend courses, vacation seminars and Teacher Trainings for those wanting to dive much deeper into these ancient teachings.   For complete course descriptions, please see our Event Calendar on the SourceTantra.com website.

BEGINNERS WEEKEND SEMINARS
Tantra: The Art of Conscious Loving®

These Friday through Sunday seminars are currently held in Santa Cruz and Santa Monica, California, as well as Ashland, Oregon. The group is gender balanced and comprised of both singles and couples. There is no nudity or partnering up required during these events. [Singles & Couples]

COURSE SUMMARY: Learn 22 Powerful tantra techniques to transform sex into profoundly deep sexual love. An experiential, transformative weekend that will Awaken consciousness as it gives you information that you will use for the rest of your life. No prior knowledge or experience is necessary.

VACATION SEMINARS & RETREATS

"Spiritual & energetic aspects of sexual loving were highlighted, along with a variety of little known exotic techniques to make one a better lover. These techniques alone were worth the price of admission." - **Common Ground Magazine**

Please check out our website at sourcetantra.com for current dates and packages available!

THE ART OF CONSCIOUS RELATIONSHIP VACATION SEMINAR • SANTA CRUZ, CA

A week of Tantric immersion with advanced practices and teachings, for all levels of Tantric seekers. [Couples Only]

Remember back to your Tantra seminar with us, and recall how you felt Sunday night. How open and connected you felt to to the group and to your Self. How excited you were about the future of your love life. Now imagine there are still 6 days to go in your seminar and you're on vacation with a group of just 20, like minded seekers.

Please see our website for other vacation seminars and special week-long events.

TANTRA TEACHER TRAININGS

After you have taken one of our beginners courses, you will be eligible to attend our Tantra Mastery seminars.

Our **Certified Tantra Educator® (CTE)** and **Advanced Certified Tantra Educator® (ACTE)** program consists of 3 levels of Tantra instructor training courses covering topics from advanced healing techniques to White Tantra meditation to teaching your own Tantra seminars.

Even if you don't want to teach Tantra to others, our CTE courses are hailed as life-changing experiential events that will have a positive effect on your sexual love-life, magnetism and ability as a healer as you move forward down your path.

CTE Level 1 takes place twice per year, with Levels 2 & 3 staggered in between those events accordingly. Please note that you must start at Level 1 and proceed through the levels in order.

Practitioners who graduate and get full certification through our program may also be eligible for being listed officially on our website! We are very proud of our CTEs, who are currently teaching Tantra and conscious sexuality in countries all over the world.

BONUS MATERIALS
Preview Our New Book
"Sacred Sexual Awakenings"

Awakening, Awareness, Transformation, Knowing

by D.J. King

At Source School of Tantra Yoga's Beginners Weekend Seminar, I opened a part of myself that has been closed down for much too long – maybe my entire life. Although I'd dabbled in Tantra for the past two years, most of my knowledge was intellectual, not experiential. And although the Muir's impart an abundance of information, it was the safe space they provided and their encouragement that made all the difference.

I came to the weekend single and was blissfully pleased, and surprised, to find that more than half the participants in the course were also single – an equal balance of men and women.

Friday night, as the singles were introduced to each other, we looked around the circle, each person, I'm certain, wondering if there would be someone in this diverse group of strangers who would help us move through our blocks, our fears, our old programs and in who would help us heal.

At the end of the evening I struck up a conversation with a man I had met briefly once before, but who I didn't really know. Over the course of the next hour and a half, we discovered we had much in common, a very unusual connection. The kind where you can talk for hours, not realizing time has slipped away.

The next day, as we chose our seats for the opening session, and as we selected partners for an exercise, he was always, magically, by chance, right in front of me or beside me. Not believing in coincidence, I began to look at the possibility of doing the Saturday night "homework" with him.

I had a lot of trepidation about doing the homework at all. A single woman picking a man, a virtual stranger, to help heal her, to help her release the life force energy from her second chakra, brought up all kinds of old programs, judgments and fears. On top of that, I had just begun the "cleansing" phase of my moon cycle and felt anything but clean. What man, what stranger, would want to deal with that mess? In my experience, this was not something men found pleasant. Even men who said they loved me, weren't able to "love" me during those five days.

But this is my year of courage and empowerment. I set that intention very clearly and strongly before the first of the year. And each time I find myself in a situation that challenges me to grow, I remember my intention. So I decided to not just step up to the precipice, but to step off, to have the faith that I would be taught to fly. I had come to the course, I had paid my money, I was going to participate fully. No more waiting for Mr. Right to come along before I do the things I want to do in my life. There is only now, and in this now I was being given an opportunity to heal. I decided to stay and to select a partner. In so doing, I stepped to the edge of the precipice.

But who would I choose? One of the female volunteers, a wonderful teacher trainee, had offered to help me if I felt I couldn't choose a man. Then, a couple, also teacher trainees, offered themselves to a single woman for the evening. Each of these options felt so much safer than choosing a man. Especially that man. He felt safe, but at the same time, the power of our connection gave me pause. I wanted to get to know him. How would that work once we had taken a step like this? Where could we go from there? Forward? No, I wasn't ready for that. It seemed too fast, too much like old pattern. Back? How do you pretend you haven't had the most intimate of experiences with someone, and go back to the "getting-to-know-you" friendship stage?

I was in a quandary. I asked spirit for guidance. "Help me choose the perfect partner," I beseeched as we began the evening ritual. The men sat in a circle, eyes closed. The women joined hands in a circle inside theirs. I placed my trust in the divine guidance, in the perfection of the universe, and moved around the circle, looking at the men who had placed themselves in such a vulnerable, yet powerful position. I didn't think about my choice as I moved in the circle. I knew I'd be shown.

The teacher asked the women to stop moving. And there I was, face to face with the perfect one. Although I had resisted, spirit, once again, magically placed that man directly in front of me.

It began slowly, nervously, like two teenagers. We talked for hours. Finally it was time, now or never. He drew me a bath and the experience began in earnest. Flowers, candlelight, incense, chocolate, Charles had instructed the men on how to set up a sacred space. And in that space, with that man, the perfect man, I stepped off the edge. And over the course of the next several hours, was taught to fly.

Using the breathing techniques that were taught to us that afternoon, and being conscious and focused, I was able to move through a phase of numbness, through deep sadness, and on to a truly spiritual experience. As he moved energy into and through my body, it began to vibrate with the energy that was being released. This was no usual sexual experience. I felt my entire body tingling, as though I had been plugged into a wall socket.

A thousand volts of electric current coursing through me, starting in my hands and feet, moving up through my arms and legs, and completely filling my torso.

It was then that I took a deep breath and pulled the energy up, focusing on my third eye. In my mind's eye, I saw an explosion of geometric white light in the space in front of my forehead and above my head. I felt loved, nurtured, cared for, cared about.

I felt the power of self expression, release, connection, oneness. At 5:00 in the morning, I fell blissfully asleep in the protective arms of a man who was a healer. My healer.

Franklin Roosevelt said, "We have nothing to fear but fear itself." Again and again I discover the profound truth of that statement. Had I not pushed through my fear, I would have lost an opportunity for profound growth. There was nothing to fear, and everything to gain.

Days later, as I ran on the beach, I noticed more people smiling at me, offering a friendly hello. Were people just friendlier today? No, I don't think so. I think it was me. I believe that this process released a tangible, transformative force, one that others, on a subtle, energetic level, are attracted to.

Now I know. I know what my teachers have been trying to tell me for years.

I deeply understand the power of life energy and what happens when we lock it away, deep inside of us. When we don't let it flow.

Grace guided me to Charles and Leah at the perfect time in my life. And I know that this practice will become an integral part of my life. A door has been opened. There is no turning back.

Goddess Unveiled

by S. Dolena

My life partner of five years, Dennis, and I decided to sign up for the Tantra Beginners Weekend towards the end of last year. We were having some relationship issues and intimacy has been non-existent for lots of reasons.

I thought if we could have an intimate weekend getting to know each other better energetically, spiritually, sensually and sexually, we might rebuild the foundation of our relationship. Dennis is the love of my life and the one with whom I want to spend the rest of my life. Unfortunately and very sadly, Dennis and I broke up before we had the opportunity to attend the workshop.

I was heart-broken and distraught. I could not see myself attending alone, as a single in this workshop. Through the encouragement of a girl friend, I did attend. I enjoyed the Tantra education, the Yoga, the breathing exercises, the intimacy exercises, the meditations and all the lovely people who were sharing themselves. But I was missing Dennis so much, especially seeing all the couples falling in love with each other again, right before my eyes. I was crying a lot. I didn't know how I was going to get through the entire weekend. I just kept breathing.

I knew the entire second day was building up to the evening Tantra healing exercise. I really did not know how this would happen as a single. Would I be matched with a stranger? Would I be able to sneak out without anyone noticing? I kept stressing and talked to my girl friend during the breaks. I began crying again. I really wanted to be here with Dennis.

When the evening came around, the couples were given their assignment and sent off to their home play. The singles were asked to stay, to sit in a circle to introduce themselves. People were given an opportunity to leave at this time. I took a deep breath and stayed. I was really curious as to what would happen next.

There will be another opportunity to leave I told myself. Then we began a lovely ceremony with the men in an outer circle facing in and women in an inner circle facing out.

The teachers were speaking to us, and their words drifted around my head like clouds that quickly melted away. I saw the men, still in a circle, sit down and close their eyes. They were told that the women would chose their partner for the evening and there were more men than women so some of them would not be chosen. They were told if they did not want to risk not being chosen, they could leave. Several men left.

Now there were more women than men. The women were also given the opportunity to leave knowing that there were now less men than women. Five women left. The suspense was intense. I took another deep breath and stayed.

We women were holding hands in our circle and began walking around in a circle, gazing upon each man, feeling their energy and asking our higher Source for guidance to select the man that would heal us that evening. I held tightly to my sisters' hands. Then Charles said, okay now stop and choose your partner. I just stood there. I could not move.

Women were moving past me and sitting in front of their chosen one. I turned around slowly and looked all around. There were women sitting in front of each man except two. There were two men sitting side by side. I thought, oh, God, how will I be able to choose. Both men looked so sweet and gentle and so trusting. So I walked over slowly to them, sat down between the two of them facing them. I took each one of their hands in mine. I had chosen both!!! I could not believe it. What was I thinking?

Then the teacher asked all the men to open their eyes and look at the Goddess that had chosen them. As they opened their eyes and looked at me, they smiled. Then they realized that I had chosen both of them. They looked at each other, then looked at me. Again, they looked at each other. I just shrugged my shoulders and said, I just couldn't choose between you, so I chose you both. What do we do now?

Well, we talked about it and decided that I would do one session with Doug first, then I would do a second session with Martin.

I went to Doug's room, and it was lovely. He had drawn a bath for me and there were candles and roses in the bathroom around the tub. Wow! I could hear soft chanting music in the background as I sank deeply into the soft, warm water of the evening. Although it felt like an eternity, it was probably twenty minutes when I emerged relaxed, warm, and fresh.

I opened the bathroom door and saw a trail of rose petals leading me into the bedroom onto the bed.

Rose petals in bed. Another Wow! We began with the "spoon position" breathing exercise. Then he asked if I would like a massage. Absolutely! As I climbed onto the bed and lay face down, I was taking off my shirt and pants just leaving on my panties. Doug was so caretaking as he massaged me. I turned over and took off my panties, and he continued to massage me all over.

As he entered to massage my sacred spot, I felt a wave of appreciation and gratitude for this man who was in service to me for my healing. I felt waves of deep loving energy flow through me. I remained in this consciousness for over an hour. Then I gently put my hand on his.

He knew I was ready to end our session. I gave him a hug and expressed my gratitude for his gift of gentle caress.

As I walked into Martin's room, all of my senses were experiencing excitement: strong, sweet incense, rhythmic chanting and music, candles, art work, pillows everywhere, and my partner in a loin cloth.

I got into bed and we began a breathing exercise. Martin began massaging me all over, and then he asked if I was ready. He entered me and found my sacred spot.

At first, I only felt pressure, then by continuing the massage, I began to feel a burning sensation in a circular spot, intense in the center and radiating with less intensity away from the center. I breathed deeply bringing my breath up my chakras as we did in the workshop exercises.

As I continued the breathing bringing our combined energies up through my body, the burning sensation melted into "almost" pleasure. I know it sounds strange.

Think of when you have an itch that needs to be scratched and you almost get to it. You get some pleasure and relief because you are close, but it is not quite on the spot. Well, that was the initial sensation.

As Martin continued massaging my sacred spot, he also massaged my breasts, my legs, my clitoris – ecstasy for my body. I began feeling the "almost" pleasure develop into definite pleasure. I kept breathing to pull the pleasure energy up through my body to my head.

My entire body began vibrating. I could feel my back arch slightly to increase the flow of pleasure.

I began to experience light-headedness so I said I needed a break. We took a breathing break sitting facing each other, he in a lotus position and me sitting on his legs with my legs around him. We held each other closely and breathed in unison.

Before we began again, he changed the music to romantic love songs. I was able to quickly get into "running" my energy again, feeling the intense pleasure and vibration. When I was not able to "take" anymore, I gently said to him, I am full.

My body was literally full and vibrating with sexual love energy. I gave Martin a hug and expressed my gratitude for the gift of sacred spot energy. I went to my room and slept soundly.

When I got up the next morning, I was still vibrating. I felt beautiful, emotionally strong and definitely cared for. I checked my cell phone which I had turned off during the workshop and evening exercise. I saw that I had three messages last night – all from Dennis.

He was telling me how much he loved me and missed me and how much he wished he was here with me. Hmmmm. Dennis and I have always had a very strong energetic connection. Maybe he could feel my energy shifting and vibrating.

The entire third day in the workshop was about healing with heart energy for both men and women. It was wonderful. I felt strong, empowered, energetic, loved and HEALED.

Yes, healed from my heartbreak.

The following week, my friends and co-workers commented on how wonderful I looked; glowing was the term they used to describe me. They were feeling a higher level of vibration from me and were attracted to it. I was getting lots of hugs and compliments. Wow!

I don't know if Dennis and I will get back together. I know that either way, I'm fine.

What I also know is that I am continuing my study of Tantra. I am Goddess power released into the universe of possibility!

Revitalizing Our Troubled Marriage

by J. Johnson

I slipped into the hot bathwater fragranced with lavender and buoyant with sea salt. My partner came near and offered to bathe me.

Squeezing water from a cloth I felt a rush of pleasure as it cascaded onto and down my body. The slightly rough washcloth found its way to my skin, stimulating and awakening my senses. I longed to extend this part of the experience, yet my body pulsed with delight at the thought of what lay ahead. In anticipation, I came out of the bath. He dried me with a soft fluffy towel and led me to the bed.

The heat of the water had raised my body temperature and I was not ready to be touched yet. So he fanned me gently with a Great Blue Heron feather. The exquisite nature of the feather touching and stroking my aura filled me with desire. I never dreamed that this gentle non-touch could send me to the height that it did. Slowly the feather reached down, touched and caressed my body, bringing me more and more pleasure with each light passage. All the while, my lover was holding my gaze, intensely being with me. Continuing to honor my need for softness and sensual pleasure he caressed me again with a small mink garment, drawing me ever higher into desire's embrace. When his hands finally found me, they were electric. As he touched me, initially without and then with movement, pleasure ran through me. The moist warmth of his mouth and the masculine quality of his hands ignited flames of passionate longing. Feeling deeply loved by his honorable entry, I opened my gates to his gently touching my sacred spot.

The first quiet movements found painful burning sensations. Ouch, ouch, ouch, then ah, ah, ah, and the chakra opened, revealing the place of pure potentiality – there, in my own sacred womb. This vision gave way to spirals of sexual ecstasy rising through my body. One orgasm after another, each longer than the last, intensity building, ebbing and flowing rolling waves of ecstatic response to the powerful surges of energy flowing through my partner to me. With and without movements on his part the waves came over and over and over again and again and again. The sound of the universe flowed from deep within, resonating out into the world, speaking volumes of emotions, releasing vestiges of pain and replacing them with the vibration of blissful happiness.

Satisfied and satiated enough for rest, we lay silent in each other's arms. As our eyes closed to each other a brilliant white light appeared in the center focus of my mind's eye. As I gazed upon this, it unfolded a multitude of tiny petals revealing a lotus blossom. And then it folded and unfolded a couple times more. This animation gave way to a vision of a path in a wood. As sleep overtook me, I accepted.

Background: The weekend Tantra Yoga experience repositioned my relationship with my husband.

Our marriage had been in a state of emotional divorce for at least eight years. We were roommates, parents and sometimes fuck buddies, living largely parallel lives. We stayed together for security of self and family, but lived with deep dissatisfaction constantly gnawing in our hearts and minds. We survived through indifference and the love I gave the same as any person whom I came in contact with. Love for the Being just because there is life. I had spent many years healing myself of the deeply ingrained trauma of long-term childhood sexual, physical, emotional, spiritual abuse and neglect. While I felt more whole, my marriage was in essence over. December came and with it the dissatisfaction gave rise to jealousy and discord.

We declared the marriage null and void and then decided to try building a different kind of relationship together. I set a deadline for re-evaluating our progress or lack thereof but I was not willing to live another 26 years with these same destructive relationship patterns.

The one area of our relationship that was even vaguely satisfying was our sex life. I thought that if anything would work for us it would be Tantra. We ordered the home study course. We both watched the DVD and I read the book, listened to the tapes, read a couple of other books and we began practicing what we understood. It was really exciting to me, as a Reiki Master and Shamanic practitioner, to relate the idea of energy flow to sexual Tantra. I saw the positions in the Kama Sutra as ways to create differing kinds of ecstatic experiences, much like trance poses to induce differing kinds of shamanic journey. As I prepared for this weekend class, I added yoga classes and took a few belly dancing classes to begin using more of my body for conducting energy in a larger way.

What I was unprepared for were the feelings of rage that began surfacing about two weeks before the class. I wasn't certain we would even make it to the workshop. My instinct was to flee. Phil was a big help in keeping me focused and in a less reactive state than I wanted to be. I saw the weekend as being a pivotal point for us. One way or the other I knew our relationship would shift over this weekend.

Needless to say, the preparations that I made paid off in a big way and I continue to have heightened sexual response. My husband has a new interest in learning to feel energy flowing and has also begun to practice White Tantra daily. I credit Reiki with my ability to feel and flow energy through my body so effectively. Red Tantra is definitely expanding my abilities and awareness exponentially.

My partner is not yet having ecstatic response, but he is beginning to recognize that he has energetic blocks and where they are. At this moment we are planning to stay the course. We are good students, doing lots of practice. Our communication skills are improving and our defensiveness is receding. Our relationship is better than it has ever been and we have real hope that we will grow in conscious loving.

CHARLES MUIR
Biography of a Tantra Master

Charles Muir is considered the originator and pioneer of the Modern Tantra Movement in the United States. In 1980, he originated the Tantra: The Art of Conscious Loving® format, Sacred Spot Massage, and many other inventive experiential exercises which have become the cornerstones in the curriculum of most Tantra educators. In addition to Red Tantra practices, Charles teaches a powerful method of White Tantra, or Laya Yoga, which is the grandfather of Hatha Yoga, with extended holds, meditation, and chakra focus. Its approach is gentle on the body, making it both relaxing and revitalizing, to awaken consciousness quickly.

Charles is quoted in over 130 books in print about sex, Tantra, relationship and yoga. He has authored 3 Tantra books, 5 Tantra Training DVDs, 3 White Tantra CDs, and 5 Red Tantra CDs. His work has been featured in over 50 media articles, numerous radio and television shows (most recently on Oprah), and 2 Hollywood feature films, Bliss and The Best Ever. He is currently working on several new projects in his Tantra: The Art of Conscious Loving series; the newest is entitled Sacred Sexual Awakenings, a comprehensive compilation of 500 testimonials and case histories of lives transformed through attending his seminars and teacher trainings.